HOW DOES MY BODY FIT TOGETHER?

...and more about the human body

CHRYSALIS CHILDREN'S BOOKS

First published in the UK in 2003 by
Chrysalis Children's Books PLC,
64 Brewery Road,
London N7 9NT

A ZIGZAG BOOK

British Library Cataloguing in Publication Data for this book is available
from the British Library.

Every effort has been made to ensure that none of the recommended
websites in this book is linked to inappropriate material. However, due
to the nature of the Internet, the publishers regret that they cannot take
responsibility for future content of the websites.

Produced by Miles Kelly Publishing Ltd
Bardfield Centre, Great Bardfield, Essex CM7 4SL

Editorial Director: Anne Marshall
Editor: Mark Darling
Copy Editor: Sarah Ridley
Indexer: Jane Parker
Proofreaders: Hayley Kerr, Leon Gray
Designer: Michelle Cannatella
Artwork Commissioning: Bethany Walker

Editorial Director, Chrysalis Children's Books: Honor Head

ISBN: 1 903954 93 2

Printed and bound in Malaysia

Contents

Make-its

3

How old was I when I was born?

People often say that the day a baby is born is the first day of its life. But a baby does not suddenly grow by magic on this day. It has already been growing for nine months, inside its mother. Every human body begins as a tiny egg cell, as small as the full stop at the end of this sentence. The egg cell grows and develops in a special part of the mother's body called the womb.

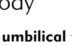

> A baby starts to smile from about six weeks old.

a baby in the womb at seven weeks

placenta

umbilical cord

fluid

at three months

bag around fluid

at six months

Bouncing babies

- Giving birth can take more than 20 hours! It is very tiring for the baby and the mother.
- More babies are born between 3 a.m. and 4 a.m. than at any other time.
- An average newborn baby weighs 3.3 kilograms. How much did you weigh when you were born?

nine months – ready to be born

INTERNET LINK
For information on babies
www.baby-place.com

> Two babies growing together in the womb are called twins.

4

← When did I grow fastest?

The body grows fastest at the beginning when it is a tiny egg cell in its mother's womb. In the first four weeks it increases in size by more than one million times. If it kept growing at this rate, then by the time it became adult it would be bigger than the whole Earth!

rolling over at three to four months

↙ Why can't a newborn baby walk and talk?

A baby needs time to learn actions such as walking and talking. A newborn baby can do very little. It sleeps a lot, feeds on milk, grasps with its fingers, and cries if it is hungry, too hot, too cold, uncomfortable or frightened.

starting to crawl at seven to eight months

cruising (walking while holding onto something) at about nine months

walking at about 12 to 16 months old

▲ *Most babies learn new actions in the same order. Some miss out a stage, for example, never crawling, but going straight from sitting to walking.*

When will I grow up?

Growth happens fast after birth. After the age of about three, growth slows down until around ten, when it speeds up again. After a time of rapid growth in the early teenage years it starts to slow again at around 14 to 16 years. The body reaches its full height by about 19 years old. Some bodies continue to grow after this, but in weight rather than height.

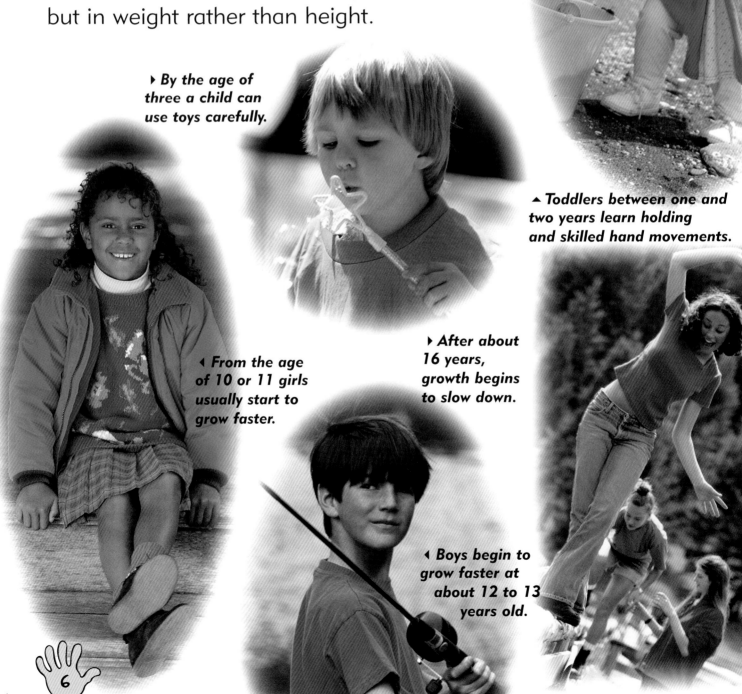

▸ *By the age of three a child can use toys carefully.*

▴ *Toddlers between one and two years learn holding and skilled hand movements.*

◂ *From the age of 10 or 11 girls usually start to grow faster.*

▸ *After about 16 years, growth begins to slow down.*

◂ *Boys begin to grow faster at about 12 to 13 years old.*

⊕ How tall will I be?

Usually, the height of a child on its second birthday is about half the height it will be when fully grown. A serious illness or lack of proper food can slow growth, although the body often catches up later. A child with two tall parents is more likely to be taller than average. Even one tall parent increases this likelihood.

QUICK QUIZ

1. If you already eat enough healthy food, but then eat more, will you grow taller?

2. Do tall parents tend to have tall children?

3. Do boys or girls stop growing first?

....

Answers – see page 32.

Is anyone average?

You will need:
some same-age friends, tape measure for height, scales for weight, pen and paper

1. Gather a group of four to six friends who are all the same age in years and measure everybody's height and weight.

2. Add up all the heights and divide by the number of friends to find the average height. Is anyone exactly average in height?

3. Then, do the same by getting everybody to weigh themselves. Is anybody average in weight?

INTERNET LINK

Find out all about your body
www.kidshealth.org

For all the issues on teenagers and their lives
www.teengrowth.com

→ Why are we ill?

There are many different kinds of illness. Some are caused by germs and are called infections, such as the common cold or a sore throat. Others may be due to accidents or injury. Often, getting an illness is just bad luck, but some are caused by lack of proper food or care. Young children should visit the health centre for check-ups even if they look well on the outside, just to check nothing is going wrong inside.

Will my skin wear away?

No! It's true that skin has to put up with a lot of wear. It gets rubbed by sponges and flannels in the shower or bathtub, then by the towel, by clothes all day and in bed at night. (And by fingernails when you have an itch.) However, the tough outer layer of skin is always growing to replace the bits that get rubbed off and flake away.

▶ *Every day, tiny flakes of skin and a few hairs fall off the body. But new ones are always growing to replace them.*

▲ *The ridge patterns of fingertip skin are called fingerprints. They are different for everyone in the world.*

Skin deep

- If you could collect all the tiny flakes of skin that rub off the body over one year, they would weigh about 4 kilograms!
- There are about 100,000 to 120,000 hairs on an average head.
- The thickest hairs on the body are usually the eyelashes.

8

How does skin feel?

Skin gives us our sense of touch and feel because it has millions of tiny touch sensors, just under its surface. These detect objects that come into contact with the skin – if they are hot or cold and whether they are soft or hard, wet or dry, moving or still. In fact, touch is very complicated!

QUICK QUIZ

1. Does the body have hairs only on the head?
2. What are the hairs called that lie between the eye and the forehead?
3. What are the hairs on a man's upper lip and chin called?

....

Answers – see page 32.

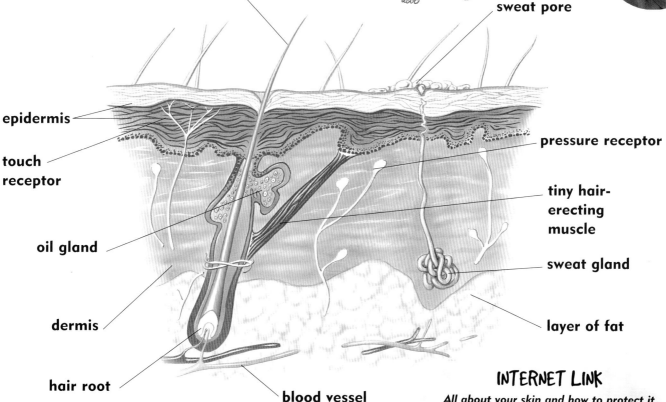

hair shaft

sweat pore

epidermis

touch receptor

pressure receptor

tiny hair-erecting muscle

oil gland

sweat gland

dermis

layer of fat

hair root

blood vessel

INTERNET LINK

All about your skin and how to protect it
www.biorap.org/br5yours.html
What to do if head lice strike!
www.bbc.co.uk/education/health/chs/headlice.shtml

Why do I have my hair cut?

To look good! Also hair would grow so long that it would be difficult to keep clean and brushed – and you might trip over it! A single head hair grows about 3 millimetres each week. After three or four years it falls out. Then a new hair usually grows in its place.

9

How does my body fit together?

All your bones are joined to form your skeleton. You need your bones, otherwise the body would flop onto the floor like a pile of jelly! The bones are the body's strong inner frame, holding up soft parts like your organs, nerves and blood vessels. They also form strong levers in the arms and legs, pulled by the muscles for movement.

skull

sternum

rib cage

humerus

radius

backbones (vertebrae)

sacrum

pelvis

femur

patella

fibula

tibia

INTERNET LINK
Discover all about the human skeleton
infozone.imcpl.org/kids_skel.htm
www4.tpgi.com.au/users/amcgann/body
/skeletal.html

▸ **There are 206 bones in the whole skeleton. Each has a medical name and many have ordinary names too. For instance, the patella is usually called the kneecap.**

⬇ Are bones completely hard?

No. Some have a heavy, very hard outer layer made of a substance called compact bone. But under this is a lighter layer with lots of holes, called spongy bone. And in the centre there's no bone at all. It's filled with marrow, which is soft like jelly and makes new parts for the blood.

marrow

compact bone

◀ Inside the end, or head, of a long bone is spongy bone. It's tough and hard, but light.

spongy bone

Bare bones

- The longest bone in the body is the femur, or thigh bone, in the upper leg.
- The smallest bone is the stirrup, deep in the ear – it's as big as this letter 'W'.
- A few people have 13 pairs of ribs, rather than 12.

➡ Why does my elbow bend?

The elbow bends so that you can put food into your mouth, scratch your neck and do hundreds of other actions. The elbow is just one of the body's many joints. A joint lets the bones slide and turn and twist – without coming apart. The bone ends are covered with shiny, smooth cartilage, so that they don't rub and wear away.

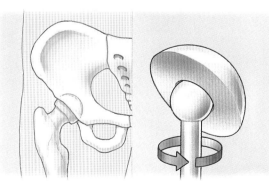

▲ The hip is a ball-and-socket design and moves many ways.

◀ The knee is like a door hinge, moving in only two ways.

11

Why is a muscle like a piece of string?

Like string it can pull, but it can't push. A muscle's job is to get shorter, or contract. It's joined to a bone at each end by a rope-like part called a tendon. As the muscle shortens, it pulls the bone and makes the body move. But a muscle cannot push. So another muscle on the other side of the bone moves it back again.

▸ *A skilled movement like hitting a ball uses many muscles in the arms and hundreds in the rest of the body to move the legs and feet and stay balanced.*

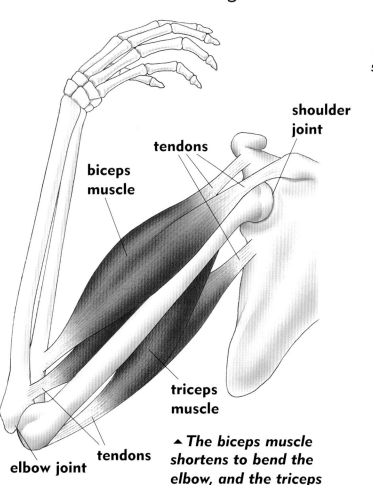

shoulder joint

tendons

biceps muscle

triceps muscle

elbow joint

tendons

▲ *The biceps muscle shortens to bend the elbow, and the triceps pulls to straighten it again.*

Muscle power

- Many of the muscles in the face are not joined to bones but to each other. You use them to make all sorts of different faces – from a grin to a grimace.
- A smile uses fewer than 20 muscles.
- A frown uses more than 40 muscles. So it's easier to smile!

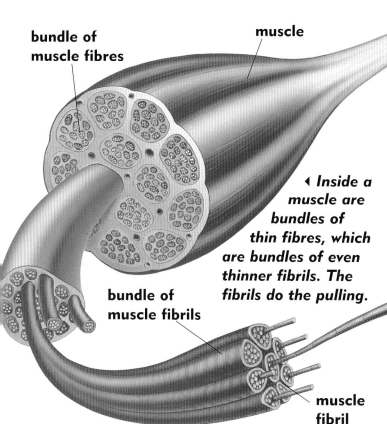

bundle of
muscle fibres

muscle

◄ *Inside a*
muscle are
bundles of
thin fibres, which
are bundles of even
thinner fibrils. The
fibrils do the pulling.

bundle of
muscle fibrils

muscle
fibril

⟲ When do my muscles go floppy?

When you lie down, rest, relax and sleep most of your muscles go soft and floppy – but not all of them. The muscles in your heart keep it beating, and those in your chest keep you breathing. As soon as you lift your head, or even one finger, the muscles are working again.

INTERNET LINK

Learn about why exercise is good for you
kidshealth.org/kid/stay_healthy/fit/work_it_out.html.

Why we cough, sneeze – and other reflex actions
www.ktca.org/newtons/13/rlxes.html

Wave bye-bye!

You will need:
safe scissors, card, sticky tape, bendy drinking straw, thread

1. Carefully cut out a hand shape (about 10 centimetres across) from the card.

2. Tape the hand to the end of the straw nearest the bendy part.

3. Tape one end of the thread halfway between the hand and the bendy part.

Imagine that the thread is an arm muscle. Pull it as shown. The elbow bends and the hand waves goodbye – or is it hi?

→ Could I count my muscles?

It would take a long time as you've got more than 650! Some are just under the skin, but some are deep inside the body, so you cannot feel them. Luckily you don't have to move each one in turn. The brain gets used to moving whole groups of them at once, automatically.

Could I live without air?

No, the body has to keep breathing fresh air to stay alive. It only needs part of air, the oxygen, which makes up about one-fifth. Oxygen is used to get energy from food, to power thousands of processes that happen every second inside the body. The parts of the body that take in air to get oxygen are the nose, windpipe and the lungs.

INTERNET LINK

Learn about lungs and breathing
www.biorap.org/br9/br9thelungs.html
Don't let asthma stop you having fun!
allergy.mcg.edu/lifequality/kac2.html

A sigh of relief

- The alveoli in your lungs are so tiny that 30 laid side by side would hardly stretch across this full stop.
- If all your alveoli were spread out flat they would cover a tennis court!
- After a race, as you pant hard, you take in and give out six times more air than you do at rest.

14

nose chamber

throat

voice box

windpipe

lung

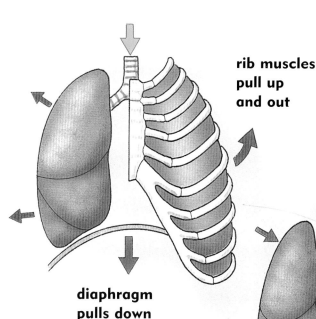

rib muscles pull up and out

diaphragm pulls down

▲ *Two sets of muscles make the lungs breathe in (above) and out (right) – the curved diaphragm under the lungs, and the rib muscles around them.*

diaphragm curves back

ribs fall back

← Do I use all the air that I breathe in?

No, you use only about one-quarter of the oxygen, which is one-twentieth of the total air breathed in. Also, the amount of air that comes out is the same as the amount that went in. This is because the body gives out a waste gas called carbon dioxide, which the lungs add to breathed-out air.

air tube (bronchiole)

→ What do I have half a billion of?

You have half a billion tiny air bubbles called alveoli deep in your lungs. Inside each one the air is very close to equally tiny blood vessels (tubes) around the alveoli. Oxygen can pass easily through the lining into the blood to be taken around the body.

blood vessels

alveoli

← Why do I cough and sneeze?

A cough is air rushing out from the lungs, up the windpipe and throat and out through the mouth. A sneeze is similar but the air comes out through the nose – at more than 150 kilometres an hour! Both these actions help to blow out bits of dust, mucus or other substances that clog or irritate the airways.

Could I live on sweets alone?

No, your body needs a wide range of foods to stay healthy, especially fresh fruits and vegetables. Lean meat, fish, eggs and milk help the body to grow at the time when it needs extra supplies of many nutrients. People who are very active need to eat plenty of energy foods, such as starches in potatoes, bread, rice and pasta.

▲ *Fruit helps your body stay healthy. It's packed with goodness, is full of juice and tastes good!*

Food for thought

- An average person eats about half a tonne of food each year, which is the weight of a family car!
- The body needs about 2½ litres of water each day.
- Most people could last for many days without food but only a day or two without water.

⭨ Why do my teeth fall out?

The body has two sets of teeth. The times when they appear vary. The first set, milk or baby teeth, usually grow from the age of about six months to three years. They fall out naturally from about six years as the adult or permanent teeth start to appear. These are bigger to fit the grown-up mouth.

3 molars
2 premolars
1 canine
2 incisors

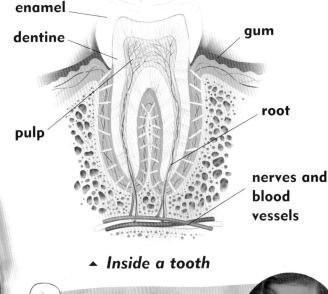

enamel
dentine
gum
pulp
root
nerves and blood vessels

▲ *Inside a tooth*

QUICK QUIZ

1. How many teeth are in the first or baby set?

2. How many teeth are in the second or adult set?

3. Which type of tooth often doesn't grow properly?

....

Answers — see page 32.

INTERNET LINK
How to make sure you have clean teeth
www.twoothtimer.com/about.htm
Fun and games on keeping your teeth healthy
www.mrreach.com

⭨ Why is the dentist my friend?

The whitish covering on your teeth, called enamel, is the hardest part of your whole body. But it must stay clean, or it goes soft, cracked and rotten. The dentist shows you how to clean your teeth properly and keep your gums and whole mouth healthy. Or would you prefer toothache?

Tooth experiment

You will need:
cola drink, some dirty coins

1. Choose two old and dull-looking coins. Put one into the cola drink. Leave the other one next to it.

2. Next day, tip out and wash the cola-coin. See how shiny and new it looks next to the other coin!

The chemicals have worn away or dissolved the surface of the coin. This is why it's so important to clean your teeth. You don't want them dissolved away!

17

Do I smell?

Yes, everyone smells – with their nose! Inside is a chamber with two hairy patches at the top. These olfactory patches detect tiny smell substances floating in air. Different hairs in each patch sense different substances, so you can detect thousands of smells, scents and odours.

▸ *Smells give you pleasure and help to bring back memories.*

Smelly facts

- Our sense of smell is about 20,000 times better than our sense of taste.
- Each olfactory patch in the nose has 25 million micro-parts called olfactory cells, to detect smells.
- An average person can tell the difference between 10,000 different smells.

▸ **Behind the nose is a large space, called the nasal cavity. The parts that smell are in its roof.**

olfactory nerve to brain

olfactory patch

nose

nasal cavity

turbinate (ridge of bone)

nostril

to throat

hard palate (floor of nasal cavity)

soft palate (roof of mouth)

⊥ How many jobs does my tongue have?

It does lots of jobs, including tasting food. A terrible taste may mean food is rotten. It helps to move food for thorough chewing. It removes bits of food from teeth. It moistens the lips so they don't dry and crack. The tongue also changes shape and position to help you speak clearly. Try to speak without moving it!

QUICK QUIZ
1. How many smells can people smell?
2. The five senses are taste, touch, smell, sight and ... what?
3. Which part of the tongue is most sensitive to touch?
....
Answers – see page 32.

▲ **Tasting foods**

▾ **Moving foods while chewing**

▲ **Cleaning bits off teeth**

▾ **Licking lips**

▲ **Speaking**

INTERNET LINK
Why nose stuff is so yukky
yucky.kids.discovery.com/flash/body/yuckystuff /snot/js.index.html
Learn more about your five senses
www4.tpgi.com.au/users/amcgann/body/senses.html

→ How does my tongue taste?

Your tongue is vital because it gives you your sense of taste. Tiny parts called taste buds detect substances in foods. The tip of the tongue detects sweet tastes best. The sides sense salty and sour flavours. The back of the tongue detects bitter tastes. The tongue is made up of very bendy muscles.

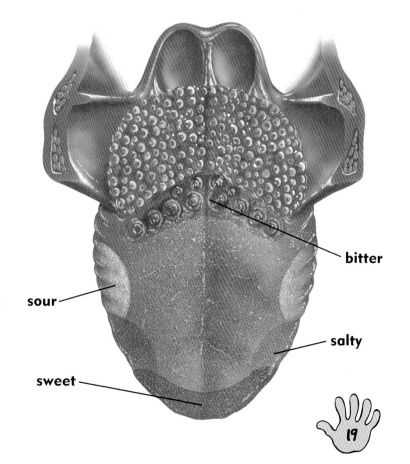

bitter

sour

salty

sweet

19

Why do my insides gurgle and rumble?

▼ *Food has a long journey through the body – it travels almost 10 metres!*

The noises are bubbles of gas inside your digestive system – the stomach and intestines (guts). These parts break down food into a mushy soup, and take the nutrients and useful substances into the body. As they add digestive juices to the food, and squeeze and squash it, gas bubbles form and gurgle along, and eventually come out at one end or the other!

1. mouth and teeth bite and chew food

2. gullet takes food to the stomach

3. stomach adds juices and churns food

4. liver stores and processes nutrients

5. pancreas makes digestive juices

6. small intestine adds more juices and takes nutrients into blood

7. large intestine takes in water and a few nutrients

8. rectum stores leftovers

9. anus lets leftovers leave body

⃕ Why does leftover food turn brown?

The food leftovers that you cannot digest leave the body as brown lumps – whatever the colour of the food you eat! This is because they contain substances other than leftover food. One is a substance from worn-out blood cells – bilirubin – which gives them their brown colour.

QUICK QUIZ

1. Which is longer, the small or large intestine?
2. What types of food help your digestive system work best?
3. Can any foods be eaten raw?

....

Answers – see page 32.

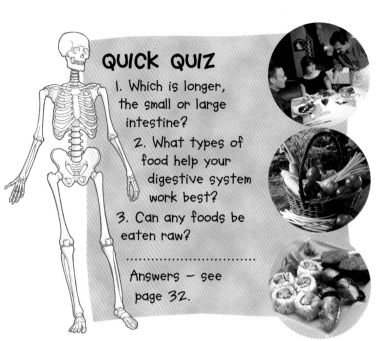

Fast food

- Food spends 2 to 6 hours in the stomach being mashed into a pulp.
- It spends 8 to 12 hours in the small intestine.
- The leftovers stay in the large intestine for 8 to 12 hours.
- On average, food's total journey through the digestive system takes 24 to 30 hours.

INTERNET LINK

Learn about eating and what happens to food www.bbc.co.uk/health/kids/eating.shtml.

Find out about your kidneys and what they make tqjunior.thinkquest.org/5777/urin1.htm

→ When is water not water?

When urine leaves the body, this is sometimes called passing water. A body system called the urinary system makes this liquid waste. Two kidneys filter blood and remove wastes and unwanted water. These pass down pipes (ureters) to be stored in the bladder, and leave the body as urine.

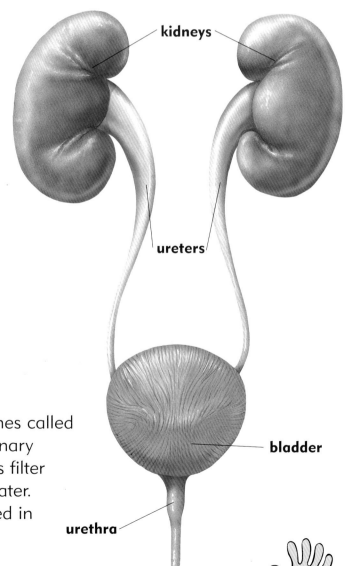

kidneys

ureters

bladder

urethra

What goes thump every second?

Your heart! Every second it squeezes hard to pump the blood inside it out through blood vessels (tubes) called arteries and around the body. The heart then relaxes and fills with more blood, coming in from vessels called veins. Then it squeezes again to pump, relaxes again to fill, and so on.

outer covering
muscle layer
stretchy layer
inner lining

red cell

plasma
platelet

white cell

main veins from head and upper body

to right lung

from right lung

to left lung

from left lung

blood in from body veins

blood in from lungs

blood out to lungs

valve

valve

blood out to body

thick muscle in heart wall

main vein

to lower body

▸ *Inside the heart are two pumps, side by side. The right pump sends blood to the lungs to collect oxygen. The left one sends it around the body.*

⬇ Why is blood red?

It contains billions of tiny red parts called red cells. These carry vital oxygen to all body parts. Blood also has white cells, which fight germs and illness. And blood has platelets, which clump together at a cut or wound. This makes the blood go lumpy or clot and seals the leak.

blood escapes through the cut

platelets go sticky and form a clot

clot hardens to a scab as the wound heals

Heart to heart

- All the body's blood vessels joined together in a long line would stretch three times round the Earth!
- Blood leaves the heart at a speed of 30 centimetres a second.
- Your heart is probably smaller than you think – about the size of your clenched fist.

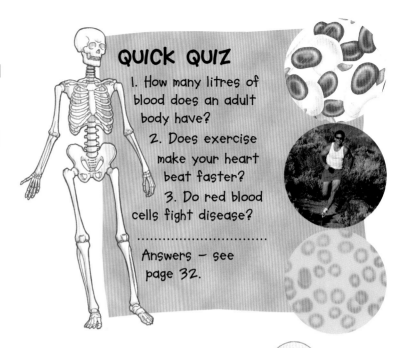

→ Where does blood flow to?

Blood does not flow to one place and stay there. It goes round and round the network of blood vessels. The smallest vessels, called capillaries, are thinner than hairs. There are thousands in every body part. Vital substances such as oxygen and nutrients can seep out of them to the parts beyond.

INTERNET LINK

What is blood and what does it do?
tqjunior.thinkquest.org/5777/cir4.htm

All about the heart and why it's so important
kidshealth.org/kid/body/heart_SW.html

Does the world disappear when I close my eyes?

No, it's still there. Even if you can't see things, you can hear, smell and touch them. Eyes give us our main sense – sight. Light shines through the dark-looking hole, the pupil, onto the inside of the back of the eye, called the retina. This detects brightness, shapes and colours, and sends signals to the brain, which then works out what the eye is seeing.

▲ *Eyes and ears give us lots of information about the world. Blocking these senses means we miss out, and may even be in danger.*

◄ *The eyeball is about 2½ centimetres across. It is protected in a bowl-shaped part of the skull bone called the eye socket or orbit.*

tough outer layer (sclera)

eyelid

cornea

retina

pupil

lens

iris

lens muscle

optic nerve to brain

jelly-like fluid (vitreous humour)

INTERNET LINK

Find out about eyes, eye tests and glasses
faculty.washington.edu/chudler/sight.html

Now hear this! All about ears and hearing
www.bbc.co.uk/health/kids/ear.shtml

Eyes can be shut – can ears?

No, ears work even when you sleep. Sounds are invisible waves in air. They pass into the hole in the ear and hit a thin piece of skin, the eardrum, making it vibrate (shake). The vibrations pass along a row of three tiny bones into a snail-shaped part called the cochlea. This detects their loudness and pitch (high or low), and sends signals to the brain, which works out what the ear is hearing.

QUICK QUIZ

1. When we say someone has brown eyes, which part is brown?

2. Can long-sighted people focus on nearby objects?

3. Do your ears or your eyes help you to balance?

....

Answers – see page 32.

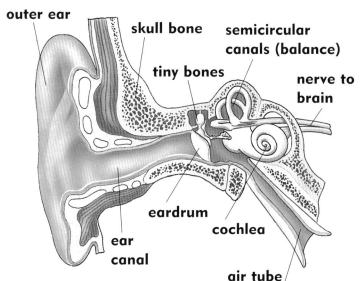

outer ear
skull bone
semicircular canals (balance)
tiny bones
nerve to brain
eardrum
cochlea
ear canal
air tube to throat

Can you believe your eyes?

Yes, usually. Sometimes we are not so sure. Optical illusions are pictures that seem to trick the eyes. Is this a vase or two people face to face? But the eyes cannot lie. They simply receive colours and patterns of light, change them into nerve signals, and send these to the brain. It's the brain that tries to make sense of the picture and in the process fools itself.

See sharp and clear
You will need:
a small clear plastic bag (like a freezer bag), water, powerful spot-beam torch

1. Part-fill the bag with water. This is like the lens in the eye. It changes shape to bend or focus light rays so they form a clear, sharp picture.

2. Shine the torch through the water-bag onto a wall just behind. Notice the shape of the beam on the wall.

3. Lower the bag onto a tabletop so it gets fatter and wider. See how the beam shape changes. The eye's lens changes shape like this to focus light rays.

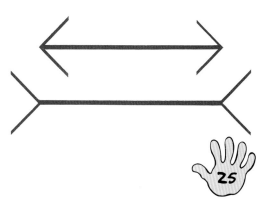

▼ *Which line is longer or are they the same? The arrows confuse the brain.*

25

Am I very nervous?

Yes, everyone is. A huge network of nerves connect all parts of the body to the brain. They look like white string and carry tiny electrical pulses called nerve messages. Nerve messages from the eyes to the brain show what the eyes see. Nerve messages from the brain to the muscles tell them to shorten and make movements.

brain

spinal cord

nerves

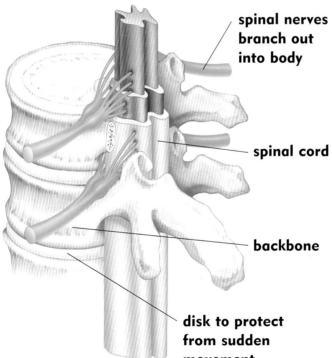

spinal nerves branch out into body

spinal cord

backbone

disk to protect from sudden movement

sciatic nerve

▲ The spinal cord is the main nerve from the brain down into the body. It is well protected in a tunnel inside the row of backbones.

▶ Nerves branch out from the brain and spinal cord to every part of the body. They carry important information between the body and the brain.

26

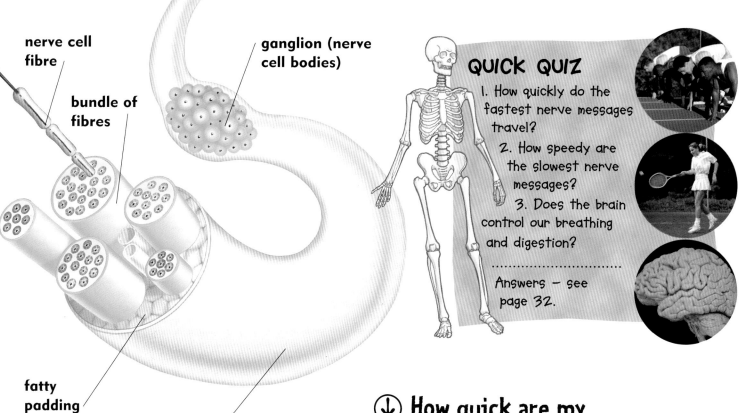

nerve cell fibre

bundle of fibres

ganglion (nerve cell bodies)

fatty padding

outer layer or sheath of nerve

QUICK QUIZ

1. How quickly do the fastest nerve messages travel?

2. How speedy are the slowest nerve messages?

3. Does the brain control our breathing and digestion?

....

Answers – see page 32.

⊼ What's inside a nerve?

A bundle of microscopic parts called nerve cells or neurons. These are too thin to see, but some are very long, more than one metre! The cells pick up nerve messages at one end, carry them along, and pass them on to other nerve cells, or to the brain or muscles.

Bag of nerves

- The thickest nerve (apart from the spinal cord) is the sciatic nerve in the hip and upper leg – it's as wide as a finger.
- The electrical signals for nerve messages are only 1/10 of a volt. (That's 1/15 the strength of a small torch battery.)
- All the body's nerves joined would stretch twice around the Earth.

⊙ How quick are my reactions?

A person can see an approaching ball, recognise what it is in the brain, work out where it's going, and tell the muscles to move the arms so that the bat hits the ball – all in less than one-fifth of a second. The nervous system is designed for fast reactions to help the body avoid danger.

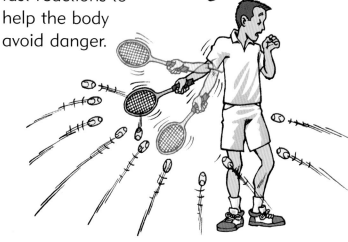

INTERNET LINK

Explore nerves and the brain with games
faculty.washington.edu/chudler/neurok.html

Loads of info on your nervous system
yucky.kids.discovery.com/noflash/body
/pg000136.html

How do I remember?

Facts and information are stored in the brain as memories. Most scientists think memories are sets of links or connections between nerve cells. If you keep recalling a fact, like your name, this reuses the links and keeps the memory strong. If not, the links get changed and the memory fades.

▲ *You can't see inside your head but a brain scan can. It uses invisible waves to take a picture of the brain inside the head.*

nerve cell body

nerve cell contacts (dendrites)

nerve cell fibre

path of nerve signal

nerve cell links (synapses)

Brain box

- An average brain weighs 1½ kilograms, which is around ⅟₅₀ of the body's total weight.
- The brain uses up to ⅕ of all the energy absorbed into the body as food.
- The brain uses ten times more energy for its size than any other body part.

◀ *In the brain, billions of nerve cells have trillions of fibres and contacts, which make zillions of links with each other. A thought or memory may be a set of nerve signals passing along certain pathways.*

⊕ Where do I think?

Where do you think you think? Your brain is the place for all thoughts, feelings, emotions, ideas and memories. It is a large, wrinkled, grey-pink lump, made of billions of tiny nerve cells. More nerve cells in nerves connect it to every body part. Different areas or centres on the brain's surface, its cortex, deal with different tasks.

movement area

touch area

taste area

hearing area

general awareness area

balance area

vision area

speech area

cerebellum

spinal cord

⊕ What happens when I sleep?

Most of your body rests and relaxes, but your brain is very busy. Yet no one knows exactly what it does. It might go through the day's events, store important information as memories, and throw away other items. The brain also dreams every hour or two. If you wake during or just after a dream you may remember it.

▼ *Most adults need between 7 and 8½ hours sleep every night, but as we get older we usually need less and less sleep.*

INTERNET LINK

Learn more about your brain and what it does
home.san.rr.com/ed4u/documents/humanbody
/page4.html
Loads of brain stuff and links
kidshealth.org/kid/body/brain_SW.html

29

Are my genes blue?

You may have some blue jeans to wear, but your body's genes are not coloured. Genes are sections of chemicals, too small to see except under a powerful microscope. The chemicals are called DNA (deoxyribonucleic acid). Genes are instructions for how the body grows, develops and carries out its life processes. Every tiny cell in the body has a set of them.

▶ *The twisted chemical DNA makes up genes.*

cell membrane (outer layer)

folded sheets or membranes inside cell

control centre of cell (nucleus)

◀ *The body is made of microscopic cells, and every cell contains genes, as well as many other tiny parts.*

INTERNET LINK
What is a gene?
www.kidshealth.org/kid/talk/qa/what_is_gene.html

↘ Where do genes come from?

From parents. When a baby begins as a tiny egg-cell, it receives one set of genes from its mother and another set from its father. Genes carry many instructions, such as how tall the person will be, whether they will be male or female, and the colour of the hair, eyes and skin. This is why a child inherits different features and looks similar to its parents. It is also why brothers and sisters may look alike.

sperm   egg

▲ *Only one sperm cell can join the egg cell to make a new human being.*

QUICK QUIZ

1. Is the full set of genes for the body called the genime, genome or genume?

2. Do my genes control the colour of my eyes?

3. Do my genes control the length of my hair?

....

Answers — see page 32.

In your genes

- Most cells in the body are less than $1/50$ of one millimetre across.
- There are 35,000 to 40,000 genes in each cell.
- All the DNA in one cell straightened and joined would stretch over 50 centimetres.

Make a new person!

You will need:
card, coloured pens, safe scissors

1. Carefully cut two head shapes from card, with ears, hair, chin and neck. Make them the same size and shape.

2. One is the mother. Draw and colour her hair, eyes, nose, mouth and other facial features.

3. The other is the father. Give him different hair, eyes and so on.

3. Their child would receive or inherit features from each parent. Cut out different parts of the two heads and put them together to make a new face. Can you see the similarities?

→ How big are genes?

Very, very, very small indeed. If you could take all the information that genes contain in chemical form, and change it into words, then you would fill more than half a million books like this one. Yet all the genes are packed into each body cell, which is 100 times smaller than this full stop.

Index

Quick Quiz answers

Page 5
1. Twins
2. Baby boys
3. About 20 hours out of 24, although this varies

Page 7
1. No
2. Yes
3. Girls

Page 9
1. No
2. Eyebrows
3. A moustache and a beard

Page 11
1. No, the enamel on teeth is harder
2. Yes, a newborn baby has more than 350 separate bones. But some of these join during growth. An adult usually has 206 bones
3. Yes, the ribs form a strong cage around the heart and lungs. The skull forms a hard case around the brain

Page 17
1. 20
2. 32

3. In some people, the wisdom teeth at the back of the mouth never appear.

Page 19
1. More than 10,000
2. Hearing
3. The tip

Page 21
1. The small intestine
2. Fruit, vegetables and cereals
3. Yes, most fruits and many vegetables, and even fish, as in the Japanese dish sushi

Page 23
1. Five
2. Yes
3. No, they carry oxygen

Page 25
1. The iris
2. No
3. Both

Page 27
1. More than 100 metres a second
2. Less than one metre a second
3. Yes

Page 29
1. Up to 100 billion neurons and even more supporting cells
2. No
3. Disorders and damage to the brain

Page 31
1. The human genome
2. Yes
3. No